# All you need to know about Kazakhstan

Copyright © 2024 Jonas Hoffmann-Schmidt. Translation: Linda Amber Chambers.

All rights reserved. This book, including all its parts, is protected by copyright. Any use outside the narrow limits of copyright law is prohibited without the written consent of the author. This book has been created using artificial intelligence to provide unique and informative content.

Disclaimer: This book is for entertainment purposes only. The information, facts and views contained therein have been researched and compiled to the best of our knowledge and belief. Nevertheless, the author and the publisher assume no liability for the accuracy or completeness of the information. Readers should consult with professionals before making any decisions based on this information. Use of this book is the responsibility of the reader.

Introduction 6

Geography and Topography 9

History before independence 12

Independence and modern history 15

Political system and government 18

Economy and trade 21

Education system and science 24

Society and population 26

Ethnic diversity and cultures 28

Traditional Clothing and Customs 30

Language diversity: Kazakh and Russian 33

Religions and beliefs 35

Architecture and urban development 37

Astana (Nur-Sultan): Capital in transition 40

Almaty: Capital of Culture and Economic Centre 43

Shymkent: Gateway to the South 46

Atyrau: The center of the oil industry 48

Uralsk: Bridge to West Kazakhstan 50

Pavlodar: Industrial hub in the east 52

Karaganda: Mining and Industrial History 55

Aktobe: Regional diversity in the west 57

Turkestan: Historical Heritage and Pilgrimage Site 60

The Silk Road: Trade Route of History 63

Modern transport infrastructure and development 66

Natural resources and environmental protection 69

Steppe and semi-desert: Ecosystems of Kazakhstan 72

Wildlife and nature reserves 74

Culinary traditions and national dishes 76

Famous Kazakh dishes and specialties 78

Music and Dance: Cultural Expressions 80

Literature and the art scene 82

Festivals and holidays 84

Sports and leisure activities 87

Nomadic culture and traditional way of life 89

Fine Arts and Crafts 92

Modern pop culture and media landscape 94

Kazakhstan in global diplomacy 97

International Relations and Partnerships 100

Tourism: Sights and Destinations 102

Must-see: National parks and natural wonders 104

Museums and historical sites 106

Outlook: Future prospects and challenges 108

Closing remarks 111

# Introduction

Kazakhstan, a country in Central Asia, fascinates with its diversity of landscapes, cultures and history. Located in the heart of the Eurasian continent, it borders Russia to the north, China to the east, Kyrgyzstan, Uzbekistan and Turkmenistan to the south, and the Caspian Sea to the west. With an area of more than 2.7 million square kilometers, Kazakhstan is one of the largest countries in the world, about nine times the size of Germany.

The history of Kazakhstan goes back a long way. Even in ancient times, nomadic tribes existed here who inhabited the vast steppe land and strongly influenced their way of life by the natural conditions. Later, the region became part of the powerful Mongol Empire and experienced various phases of rule, including the Golden Horde period. In the 15th century, the area came under the influence of rulers from Central Asia and the Orient, which further enriched the cultural diversity of the country.

In the 18th century, Russian expansion to the south began, and Kazakhstan became part of the Russian Empire. This period brought fundamental changes, including the introduction of Christianity and later Islam. With the revolution of 1917 and the collapse of Tsarist Russia, Kazakhstan became part of the Soviet Union and received the status of an autonomous Soviet republic. During the Soviet era, the country experienced rapid industrialization and urbanization, with cities such as Almaty and Astana (now Nur-Sultan) growing into significant centers.

Kazakhstan's independence was declared in 1991 after the collapse of the Soviet Union. Since then, the country has developed into a stable republic that shapes its political, economic and cultural identity. The transition to a market economy and the modernization of infrastructure characterize the current phase of Kazakhstan's history. The country is rich in natural resources, especially oil and gas, which has contributed to economic development and the establishment of international relations.

Culturally, Kazakhstan is a melting pot of different ethnicities and religions. Kazakhs form the largest ethnic group, but Russians, Ukrainians, Tatars, Germans and many other peoples also shape the diversity of the country. The cultural scene is rich in traditional music, dance, crafts and culinary delights. The Kazakh language, closely related to Turkmen and Kyrgyz, is the official language of the country, while Russian is widely spoken and used in many areas of public life.

With a rich history, a unique natural environment and a dynamic development in the present, Kazakhstan offers countless facets to discover and understand. This introduction offers a first insight into the complexity of this fascinating country and paves the way for the further chapters, which will offer deeper insights into the various aspects of Kazakhstan.

## Geography and Topography

Kazakhstan, the ninth largest country in the world, is located in the central part of Eurasia and covers an area of more than 2.7 million square kilometers. It is bordered by Russia to the north, China to the east, Kyrgyzstan, Uzbekistan and Turkmenistan to the south, and the Caspian Sea to the west. This geographical location makes Kazakhstan an important crossroads between Europe and Asia.

The topography of Kazakhstan is extremely diverse, ranging from endless steppes and semi-deserts to high mountain ranges and the unique Caspian Sea in the west. In the north, the vast steppes of the Eurasian Steppe, which extend to the Russian border, dominate. This region is characterized by rolling hills that are ideal for the nomadic livestock farming traditionally practiced by the Kazakh tribes.

In the south, the country extends to the foothills of the Tianshan Mountains and the Altai Mountains, which partly form the border with China. Here you will find spectacular landscapes with deep gorges, picturesque mountain lakes and high peaks that can reach over 4,000 meters high. The highest mountain in Kazakhstan is Khan

Tengri with an altitude of 7,010 meters, which is located in the Tian Shan Mountains and is a destination for mountaineers from all over the world.

The Caspian Sea in western Kazakhstan is the largest inland body of water in the world and an important ecological and economic center of the region. It is surrounded by fertile lowlands, which play an important role in the country's agricultural production. This region is also rich in oil and natural gas deposits, which have made Kazakhstan one of the largest energy producers in the world.

The central and eastern regions of Kazakhstan consist mainly of semi-deserts and steppes that extend over long distances. Dry plains and hilly landscapes dominate here, but despite the apparent drought, they have a rich biodiversity. There are numerous nature reserves and game reserves that protect the country's diverse wildlife, including rare species such as the saiga antelope and the snow leopard.

The climate in Kazakhstan varies greatly depending on the region. While the north has a continental climate with cold winters and warm summers, the south is characterized by a dry continental climate that tends to have hot summers and cold winters. In the mountainous regions, temperatures can be extreme, with strong temperature differences between day and night.

Overall, Kazakhstan's geographical diversity provides an impressive backdrop for its rich history, cultural diversity, and economic development. The country's landscapes reflect its complex identity and offer a wealth of opportunities for exploration and discovery.

## History before independence

Kazakhstan has a rich and complex history that dates back well before the country's independence in 1991. The origins of civilization in this area date back to ancient times, when nomadic tribes inhabited the vast steppes and semi-deserts. These nomadic peoples developed a unique culture that was strongly influenced by the natural conditions of the region. Horse breeding and livestock breeding were central elements of their way of life, allowing them to survive and develop in a seemingly inhospitable environment.

In ancient times, the territory of today's Kazakhstan was part of the Scythian Empire, a people of equestrian nomads who ruled throughout the Eurasian steppe. The Scythians left behind impressive archaeological remains, including well-preserved royal tombs with golden treasures and artwork that showcased their advanced craftsmanship.

Over the centuries, various civilizations and conquerors came to Central Asia. In the 4th century BC, the area was conquered by Alexander the Great and came under the influence of Hellenism. Later, in the 8th century, Islamic expansion came to the region, bringing Islam as the dominant religion. Muslim culture and architecture left a lasting mark and influenced the society and daily life of the people of Kazakhstan.

From the 13th century onwards, the Mongol Empire under Genghis Khan and later under his successors exerted great influence on Central Asia. Kazakhstan became part of the Golden Horde, one of the sub-kingdoms of the Mongol Empire that ruled the area until the 15th century. This period shaped the political landscape and economic relations in the region and laid the foundation for cultural exchange between Asia and Europe along the Silk Road.

In the 15th century, Kazakhstan came under the influence of the Uzbek khans from neighboring Transoxania, who ruled the region until Russian expansion in the 18th century. During this time, Russia began to expand its southern borders, and Kazakhstan eventually became part of the Russian Empire. This era brought profound changes, including the introduction of Christianity in some regions and later the dominance of Russian as an administrative language.

With the October Revolution of 1917, Kazakhstan became part of the Soviet Union and received the status of an autonomous Soviet republic. During the Soviet era, the country experienced rapid industrialization and urbanization, with major cities such as Almaty and later Astana (now Nur-Sultan) growing as important political and economic centers.

The history of Kazakhstan before its independence is shaped by a variety of peoples, cultures and influences, which together have created a rich cultural and historical landscape. This development formed the basis for the country's modern identity and still influences its political, economic and social development today.

# Independence and modern history

After the dissolution of the Soviet Union in 1991, Kazakhstan gained its independence as a sovereign state. This marked a significant turning point in the country's history and set the framework for a new era of political, economic and social transformation. Nursultan Nazarbayev became the first president of Kazakhstan and led the country through the difficult phase of the transition from a communist to an independent state.

In the early years of independence, Kazakhstan focused on building its own state institutions and creating a new, constitution that laid the foundation for democratic principles and the rule of law. Economic reforms were initiated to lead the country from the centralized, planned economy of the Soviet era to a market economy. This transition was challenging and fraught with economic difficulties as Kazakhstan sought to integrate into the global economy and use its natural resources effectively.

The 1990s were marked by social change and economic restructuring. The privatization of companies and the creation of new economic sectors such as energy and mining contributed to the diversification of the economy. Kazakhstan has rich oil and gas reserves in the west of the country, especially in the Caspian Sea, which gave the country a strategic role in the global energy sector.

The construction of the new capital Astana, which was later renamed Nur-Sultan, symbolized Kazakhstan's will to become a modern and forward-looking nation. Urban development became a central element of the national identity, reflecting the country's architectural style and cultural and political ambitions.

Politically, Kazakhstan pursued a policy of multilateral diplomacy and sought a balanced foreign policy that maintained good relations with its neighbors in Central Asia, Russia, China, and the West. The country played an active role in international organizations such as the United Nations and the Organization for Security and Cooperation in Europe (OSCE), which contributed to its position as a major player on the global stage.

The turn of the millennium brought further challenges and opportunities for Kazakhstan. The government increasingly relied on educational reforms to improve the quality of education and prepare the young generation for the demands of the global economy. At the same time, the country focused on promoting investment in infrastructure projects to promote economic development in remote areas and improve the quality of life of the population.

In recent decades, Kazakhstan has continued to experience dynamic changes and remains committed to strengthening its national identity and consolidating its role in the global community. Advances in economic diversification, the promotion of social development and the strengthening of democratic institutions form the basis for the future of the country in the 21st century.

# Political system and government

Kazakhstan's political system is defined by its 1995 Constitution, which establishes fundamental principles of democracy and the rule of law. According to this constitution, Kazakhstan is a presidential republic in which the president acts as the head of state and the highest executive officer. The president is directly elected by the people for a five-year term and can serve a maximum of two consecutive terms.

Legislative power lies with the parliament, known as the "Maslikhat". The parliament consists of two chambers: the lower house, called the Majilis, and the upper house, called the senate. The members of the Majilis are elected every five years, with half of the seats allocated in proportion to the results of the party list elections and the other half in individual constituencies. The Senate consists of two members from each of Kazakhstan's 14 administrative districts and the capital, appointed by the president.

The political system is characterized by strong presidential power, with the president playing a significant role in setting the political agenda and national policy. The president appoints the prime minister and can dismiss the cabinet as well as make important political decisions, including foreign policy and security issues.

Kazakhstan's legal system is based on civil law, which is heavily influenced by Soviet legal principles. However, the independence of the judiciary remains a controversial issue, as political influences on court decisions have been observed. Kazakhstan is a member of various international organizations, including the United Nations, the Organization for Security and Cooperation in Europe (OSCE), and the Shanghai Cooperation Organization (SCO).

Kazakhstan's political landscape is dominated by several political parties, but only a few of them play a significant role. The Nur-Otan Party, which is considered the ruling party, dominates the political scene, followed by other parties such as the Ak Zhol Party and the Communist People's Party of Kazakhstan. Despite formal multi-party elections, there are concerns about the actual political diversity and fairness of elections.

In recent years, Kazakhstan has taken steps to advance political and economic modernization and strengthen its institutions. This includes efforts to fight corruption, promote the rule of law and improve transparency in governance. The future of Kazakhstan's political system will be shaped by internal and external challenges as the country continues on its path to strengthening democracy and promoting economic prosperity.

# Economy and trade

The economy of Kazakhstan has developed dynamically since its independence in 1991 and is now one of the largest and most advanced in Central Asia. The country benefits greatly from its rich natural resources, especially oil and gas, which make it a significant player in the global energy market. Kazakhstan has enormous reserves of raw materials, including coal, metals and rare earths, which are important exports.

The energy sector is the backbone of Kazakhstan's economy and contributes a significant part of the gross domestic product. Large oil and gas fields, especially in the western part of the country around the Caspian Sea, are crucial for energy production. Kazakhstan is one of the world's largest oil exporters and has significant partnerships with international energy companies to develop and process its resources.

In addition to the energy sector, the mining industry plays an important role in Kazakhstan's economy. The country is rich in raw materials such as uranium, zinc, copper, and other metals, which are mined on a large scale. The extraction and processing of minerals is an important economic sector and contributes to the industrial development of the country.

The agricultural sector also remains of great importance, although it contributes less to economic output compared to raw materials and energy. Kazakhstan has fertile soils in some regions that are used for the cultivation of wheat, barley, cotton and other agricultural products. Livestock farming, especially sheep and cattle, is also widespread and an important part of traditional economic activities in rural areas.

In recent years, Kazakhstan has made considerable efforts to diversify its economy and promote other sectors such as information technology, telecommunications, and tourism. The government has taken measures to attract foreign investment and modernize the country's infrastructure, including the expansion of transport routes and the development of special economic zones.

Trade plays a central role in Kazakhstan's economy, with Russia, China and the EU being the main trading partners. The country is a member of the Eurasian Economic Union (EAEU), which promotes trade and economic cooperation with its neighboring countries.

Kazakhstan is actively seeking to diversify its trade relations and expand its export markets in order to reduce its dependence on raw materials and promote sustainable economic development.

Despite this progress, Kazakhstan still faces challenges, including the need to further diversify its economy, fight corruption, promote entrepreneurship, and ensure an equitable distribution of economic benefits in the country. The future of Kazakhstan's economy depends on its ability to address these challenges and take advantage of the opportunities presented by its strategic location and natural resources.

## Education system and science

Kazakhstan's education system has developed continuously since independence in 1991, with the government making great efforts to improve the quality and accessibility of education in the country. The education system is divided into several levels, including kindergarten, primary, secondary, and higher education.

Primary education begins at the age of six and includes a compulsory nine years of schooling. Secondary education is divided into two cycles: a four-year tenth grade cycle and a two-year eleventh and twelfth cycle. After completing secondary education, students have the option of either pursuing vocational training or entering the higher education system.

Kazakhstan's higher education system includes a variety of state and private institutions that offer a wide range of study opportunities. The leading universities in the country are the Kazakh National University Al-Farabi in Almaty, the Kazakh National Technical University in Almaty and the Eurasian National University L.N. Gumilev in Nur-Sultan. These institutions offer degree programs in various fields, including science, engineering, humanities, medicine, and economics.

Kazakhstan has also made efforts to promote scientific research and development. Government programs and government funding support projects in areas such as energy, environmental protection, agriculture, and information technology. Research institutions and institutes work closely with universities to drive innovation and contribute to the country's economic development.

The government has taken initiatives to promote international cooperation in education and science, including student and scholar exchanges and participation in international research projects and programs. Kazakhstan is a member of various international educational organizations and strives to integrate into the global education space.

Despite this progress, Kazakhstan's education system continues to face challenges, including the need for further modernisation of curricula, improving teacher training and ensuring quality assurance in education. Promoting education remains a key goal for the government, as it contributes to the development of a well-educated and competitive workforce and forms the basis for sustainable economic growth in Kazakhstan.

## Society and population

Kazakh society is characterized by a rich cultural diversity and a history of nomadic traditions that dates back to ancient times. The country's population is ethnically diverse, with Kazakhs making up the largest group, followed by Russians, Ukrainians, Uzbeks, Tatars, and other minorities. This diversity is reflected in the language, culture and way of life of the people.

Traditional Kazakh society was nomadic, with livestock and nomadism playing a central role in people's lives. Although modern Kazakhstan has evolved into an urbanized society, many elements of nomadic traditions and customs remain to this day, especially in rural areas.

Religion plays a significant role in the lives of Kazakhs, with Islam being the dominant religion. Most of the population practices Sunni Islam, while there is also a small community of Shiites. In addition to Islam, there are Christian minorities, especially Russian Orthodox Christians, as well as small groups of Buddhists and followers of other faiths.

The family structure in Kazakhstan is traditionally strong and focused on mutual support. Large families are common, with several generations living under one roof.

Respect for older family members and the cultivation of traditional values such as hospitality and honor are deeply rooted in Kazakh culture.

Urbanization has increased in recent decades, with the cities of Almaty and Nur-Sultan being the largest metropolitan areas in the country. These cities function as economic, political, and cultural centers that offer a modern way of life and a variety of educational and work opportunities.

Kazakhstan is a multilingual country where Kazakh and Russian are the main official languages. Kazakh is the official state language, while Russian is widely spoken and used in administration, education, and media. Multilingualism is a central feature of society and contributes to the cultural diversity of the country.

The challenges of social development in Kazakhstan include managing urban migration, improving health care and educational opportunities in rural areas, and promoting gender equality and minority rights. The government strives to address these challenges and promote an inclusive society based on mutual respect and social justice.

## Ethnic diversity and cultures

Kazakhstan is known for its impressive ethnic diversity and cultural complexity, which is the result of a rich history of migration, trade, and political change. The largest ethnic group is the Kazakhs, who make up a significant part of the population and have a deep connection to the country's nomadic past. Their culture is shaped by traditional customs such as nomadism, livestock farming and the art of carpet making, all of which play a central role in daily life.

In addition to the Kazakhs, there is a sizable Russian minority, whose presence dates back to the time of Russian colonization and the Soviet era. Russians have left significant cultural and linguistic influences and are active in many areas of social life, especially in cities such as Almaty and Nur-Sultan.

Other ethnic groups in Kazakhstan include Ukrainians, Tatars, Uzbeks, Kyrgyz, Germans, and many more who came to the country for various historical and geographical reasons. This diversity is reflected in the languages, customs, religions and culinary traditions that together contribute to the cultural landscape of the country.

Religious diversity is also a feature of Kazakhstan, with Islam being the dominant religion. The majority of Muslims practice Sunni Islam, while there is also a small Shiite community. In addition to Islam, there are Orthodox Christians, Buddhists and followers of other faiths, who represent a rich religious mix in the country.

Kazakhstan's cultural scene is dynamic and diverse, with traditional art forms such as music, dance, crafts, and literature playing a significant role. Kazakh music is known for its traditional instruments such as the dombra and its melodic patterns, which often reflect the history and nature of the steppe. Kazakh dances such as the "Kara Zhorga" and "Shapan" are expressions of joy, celebration and community spirit.

The Government of Kazakhstan has made efforts to promote and preserve the country's cultural diversity by supporting initiatives that promote the traditions and languages of ethnic minorities. Nevertheless, challenges such as the integration of ethnic minorities into social and economic life and the preservation of cultural identity remain. Kazakhstan remains committed to preserving its cultural heritage while promoting an inclusive and harmonious society that considers diversity as a strength.

# Traditional Clothing and Customs

The traditional clothing and customs associated with it in Kazakhstan are a living testimony to the country's rich cultural history and nomadic traditions. The Kazakhs, the largest ethnic group in Kazakhstan, have a unique traditional clothing that is closely linked to their nomadic way of life. Men often wear long, loose-fitting robes known as "chapan," along with high felt hats called "tubeteika." These clothes are not only functional and protect against the extreme climatic conditions of the steppe, but also symbolize the cultural identity and pride of the Kazakhs.

Women traditionally wear long, ornate dresses known as "Saukele," often with richly embroidered patterns and decorative elements. Headgear such as "takiya" or "elechek" are also important components of women's traditional clothing and symbolize the role of women in the family and community.

In addition to the Kazakhs, other ethnic groups in Kazakhstan have also developed their own traditional clothing styles and customs. Russians and other Slavs often wear traditional clothing on special occasions or festivals that have their cultural roots in Russian history and tradition. Tatars, Uzbeks, and Kyrgyz also have distinctive clothing styles and jewelry traditions that reflect their ethnic identity.

Traditional customs in Kazakhstan include a variety of festivals, rituals and celebrations celebrated throughout the year. One example is the "Nowruz" festival, which marks the beginning of spring and the new year in the Persian calendar and is widely celebrated in Central Asia. Other traditional festivals include weddings, births, religious holidays, and cultural events that provide opportunities to strengthen community and strengthen cultural ties.

Traditional music and dance are also essential components of Kazakh culture. Musical instruments such as the dombra, a two-stringed lute, are often played on festive occasions and events, accompanied by traditional dances such as the "Kara Zhorga", which reflects the grace and vitality of the nomadic way of life.

The preservation and promotion of traditional clothing and customs remains an important concern in Kazakhstan, as they not only strengthen cultural identity, but also preserve the pride and heritage of the population. Modern developments have led to the fusion of traditional elements with contemporary fashion and way of life, striking a balance between preservation and adaptation to preserve the country's cultural diversity.

## Language diversity: Kazakh and Russian

The linguistic diversity in Kazakhstan reflects the country's complex ethnic and cultural landscape. Kazakh and Russian are the two official languages of the country, with Kazakh acting as the state language and Russian as the language of interethnic communication. Kazakh belongs to the Turkic-speaking group and is closely related to other Central Asian languages such as Kyrgyz and Uzbek. It is spoken by the vast majority of the Kazakh population and is an integral part of Kazakhstan's national identity.

Russian has a long history in Kazakhstan and was widely used as an administrative and educational language during the period of Russian colonization and the Soviet era. Despite Kazakhstan's independence and the promotion of Kazakh as the state language, Russian remains an important language in public life, especially in cities and in areas such as education, business, and media.

In addition to Kazakh and Russian, there are a variety of other languages spoken by the country's ethnic minorities. These include Ukrainian, Uzbek, Tatar, German, and other languages that are widely spoken depending on ethnic and regional conditions. The

Government of Kazakhstan supports the promotion and protection of linguistic diversity in the country through laws and programs that promote the use and development of the languages of ethnic minorities.

Multilingualism is an essential feature of public life in Kazakhstan, with many people being able to speak several languages fluently. This linguistic diversity contributes to the cultural and social dynamics of the country and promotes intercultural exchange and understanding between different population groups.

The promotion of Kazakh as a state language is an important concern of the government, as it contributes to strengthening national identity and consolidating the country's independence. At the same time, the importance of Russian as a bridging language between different ethnic groups and as a means of international communication is recognized.

Language policy in Kazakhstan remains a dynamic issue as the country strives to strike a balance between promoting the Kazakh language and upholding the rights of linguistic minorities. This process reflects efforts to preserve the country's cultural diversity while strengthening national unity and social cohesion.

# Religions and beliefs

Religions and beliefs play an important role in Kazakhstan's diverse religious landscape. Islam is the dominant religion in the country, with the majority of the Muslim population belonging to Sunni Islam. This religious tradition has deep roots in the history of Kazakhstan and is closely linked to the cultural identity of the Kazakh community. Mosques serve as religious centers and are places of prayer, education, and social interaction for Muslims in urban and rural communities.

In addition to Islam, there are a variety of other religious beliefs in Kazakhstan. A significant minority of the population practices Russian Orthodox Christianity, which was introduced to the country during the period of Russian colonization and the Soviet era. Orthodox churches are present in many cities and rural communities and play an important role in the religious life of the Russian-speaking population.

In addition, there are smaller religious communities, including Catholics, Protestants, and Jehovah's Witnesses, each of which has a small but dedicated following. These religious minorities practice their beliefs freely and have the right to express their religious beliefs publicly.

In addition to the traditional religions, there are also a smaller number of Buddhists in Kazakhstan, especially among the ethnic groups such as the Kalmyks and Tuvans, who come from the Buddhist tradition of Central Asia. These communities have their own temples and spiritual centers that play an important role for believers.

Freedom of religion is guaranteed in the Constitution of Kazakhstan, and the government supports the promotion of interreligious harmony and the protection of religious minorities. Interreligious dialogue and cooperation are important components of social life, with religious leaders and communities coming together regularly to discuss common concerns and contribute to the promotion of social peace.

Despite the diversity of religious beliefs in Kazakhstan, society as a whole is characterized by a spirit of tolerance and respect for different faiths. The promotion of religious plurality and the recognition of the cultural contributions of different religious communities are central elements of national identity and contribute to strengthening social cohesion in Kazakhstan.

# Architecture and urban development

Kazakhstan's architecture and urban development reflect a fascinating mix of traditional influences, Soviet planning, and modern design. The country's urban landscape is characterised by a combination of historic buildings, Soviet prefabricated buildings and contemporary skyscrapers that characterise the urban image.

Cities such as Almaty, the former capital, and the new capital, Nur-Sultan (formerly Astana), are home to architectural masterpieces that combine modern technology and traditional design. Almaty, nestled in the picturesque backdrop of the Tien Shan Mountains, showcases a mix of Soviet architecture from the Stalin era and modern residential high-rises and business centers that dominate the cityscape.

Nur-Sultan, on the other hand, is an example of modern urban design and has become an architectural showcase project in recent decades. The city is known for its skyscrapers, including the Bayterek Tower, which is a symbol of Kazakhstan's independence, as well as its futuristic architecture designed by renowned architects.

Historic cities such as Taras, Shymkent, and Oskemen showcase a variety of architectural styles and structures that reflect the history and cultural development of the region. Traditional Kazakh construction, often made of clay and wood, can be seen especially in rural areas and historic villages, where ancient fortresses and mausoleums still stand.

Kazakhstan's urban development has been shaped by economic investments and policy decisions aimed at modernizing the country and improving the quality of life of its residents. Infrastructure projects such as road construction, public transport and urban renewal are key factors in the further development of cities and the promotion of economic growth.

Architecture plays an important role in defining Kazakhstan's urban identity and cultural heritage. The government strives to preserve historic buildings and protect architectural heritage, while promoting new construction projects that reflect the modern way of life and help create a sustainable urban environment.

The future of architecture and urban development in Kazakhstan faces challenges such as coping with population growth, sustainability in construction and preserving cultural identity in a globalized world. Through balanced planning and the promotion of innovative architectural projects, Kazakhstan strives to make its cities centers of social, economic and cultural progress that reflect the diversity and beauty of the country.

## Astana (Nur-Sultan): Capital in transition

Astana, now known as Nur-Sultan, is one of the youngest capitals in the world and an outstanding example of urban development and architectural innovation. The city is located in the north of Kazakhstan and was declared the capital in 1997 when it was called Astana. The name was changed to Nur-Sultan in 2019 in honor of former President Nursultan Nazarbayev.

The development of Astana into Nur-Sultan was a deliberate move by the Kazakh government to diversify the country economically and promote the development of the central and northern parts of the country. The city was strategically built in the steppe to maximize the potential as a connection point between Europe and Asia, symbolizing a new era of prosperity and modernity for Kazakhstan.

The architecture of Nur-Sultan is a mix of modern skyscrapers, unique government buildings, and public squares designed by internationally renowned architects. The Bayterek Tower, a symbol of the city, symbolizes the mythical tree of life and offers panoramic views of the city and the surrounding steppe from its top.

The city is also home to the Khan Shatyr Entertainment Complex, one of the largest tent structures in the world, which serves as a shopping mall, theme park, and event venue all year round. Nur-Sultan's modern design and innovative architectural elements reflect its ambition to create a city of the future that is both functionally and aesthetically impressive.

Nur-Sultan is not only a political center, but also an important economic and cultural center. The city is home to international companies, embassies, and cultural institutions, as well as a growing number of educational institutions and research centers. This has helped Nur-Sultan become a major hub for business travel and international conferences.

Nur-Sultan's urban infrastructure includes modern transportation systems, such as roads, bridges, and Nur-Sultan International Airport, which plays an important role in the region's air traffic. The government continuously invests in the development of urban infrastructure to improve the quality of life of residents and position the city as an attractive location for investment and tourism.

The future of Nur-Sultan lies in continuing to promote sustainable urban development, preserving cultural heritage and creating a dynamic urban environment that takes into account the needs of the growing population and the challenges of climate change. The city remains a symbol of Kazakhstan's progress and ambitions in the 21st century, while further strengthening its role as a capital in transition.

# Almaty: Capital of Culture and Economic Centre

Almaty, located in the southeastern part of Kazakhstan, is a city of historical importance, cultural diversity and economic dynamism. As the former capital of the country until 1997 and still the largest urban center, Almaty plays a central role in the social, economic and cultural life of Kazakhstan.

The city is picturesquely located at the foot of the Tien Shan Mountains and offers a breathtaking backdrop for its architectural and cultural diversity. Historically, Almaty was a major trading center on the ancient Silk Road and has developed into a modern economic center with a thriving trade and finance industry. The city is known for its green spaces, parks and gardens, which provide an oasis of calm in the midst of the busy city life.

Almaty is also a major cultural center of Kazakhstan, with a rich history of art, music, and literature. Numerous museums, theaters and art galleries enrich the city's cultural scene and offer insights into Kazakh culture as well as international art movements. The Almaty Opera and Ballet Theater is known for its outstanding performances and attracts visitors from all over the world.

Almaty's architecture reflects a mix of Soviet influences, modern urbanization, and traditional Kazakh architecture. Historic buildings from the time of the Tsarist rule and the Soviet era stand next to modern skyscrapers and shopping malls that characterize the cityscape. Zenkov Cathedral, a landmark of the city, is an example of the remarkable wooden construction traditionally used in the region.

Economically, Almaty is a major center for banking, financial services, commerce, and education. International companies have their headquarters here and contribute to Kazakhstan's economic development. The city is also home to prestigious educational institutions such as Al-Farabi Kazakh National University and is an important educational center for students from home and abroad.

Almaty's urban infrastructure includes modern transport systems, including a well-developed road network and Almaty International Airport, which plays an important role in the region's air traffic. The government continuously invests in the development of the city in order to improve the quality of life of residents and strengthen Almaty as an attractive location for investment and tourism.

The future of Almaty lies in promoting sustainable development, preserving cultural heritage and creating a dynamic urban environment that takes into account the needs of a growing population and the challenges of the 21st century. The city remains a symbol of Kazakhstan's progress and cultural diversity and contributes to strengthening its role as the country's cultural capital and economic center.

## Shymkent: Gateway to the South

Shymkent, the third largest city in Kazakhstan, is considered the gateway to the south of the country and plays a crucial role as an economic and cultural center in the region. The city is located near the Uzbek border and benefits from its strategic location on the trade routes between Central Asia and the Middle East. Historically, Shymkent was an important trading center on the ancient Silk Road, which has led to a diverse cultural and ethnic composition of the population.

The city's architecture reflects a mix of Soviet heritage, traditional Kazakh architecture, and modern urban planning. Historic buildings from the colonial era and the Soviet era stand next to new residential and commercial complexes that characterize the modern cityscape. The city government strives to preserve and restore historic buildings while promoting new construction projects to improve economic growth and the quality of life of residents.

Economically, Shymkent is an important industrial center focused on mechanical engineering, chemical industry, food processing and textile production. The city is home to numerous industrial plants and production facilities that contribute to the economic development of the region. The export of agricultural products and industrial goods plays an important role in the local economy.

Culturally, Shymkent is a melting pot of different ethnic groups, including Kazakhs, Uzbeks, Russians, Tatars, and many others. This diversity is reflected in the city's art, music, literature and traditions. Shymkent is known for its vibrant cultural scene, including theatrical performances, concerts, and festivals that take place throughout the year, attracting visitors from all over the region.

The urban infrastructure includes modern transport systems such as roads, bridges and Shymkent International Airport, which plays an important role in the region's air traffic. The government continuously invests in improving infrastructure to support the growth of the city and improve the quality of life of its residents.

The future of Shymkent lies in promoting sustainable development, diversifying the economy and creating a dynamic urban environment that meets the needs of a growing population. The city remains an important gateway to the south of Kazakhstan and contributes to strengthening its role as a major economic and cultural center in the region.

## Atyrau: The center of the oil industry

Atyrau, a city in the western part of Kazakhstan, plays a central role as the heart of the country's oil industry. Located on the banks of the Ural River, Atyrau is strategically positioned and serves as an important center for the exploration, production and processing of crude oil and natural gas in the region. The city is known for its significant oil fields and oil refineries, which make a significant contribution to Kazakhstan's economy.

The oil industry is the main engine of Atyrau's economy and contributes significantly to the country's gross domestic product. International energy companies have made significant investments in the region to develop and exploit the rich energy resources. Atyrau is a hub for the extraction and transportation of petroleum, with pipelines connecting the country to its neighboring countries and international markets.

In addition to the oil industry, Atyrau also plays an important role in the petrochemical industry. The city is home to numerous facilities for processing petroleum and producing petrochemical products such as plastics, fertilizers, and other chemical compounds.

These industries create jobs and contribute to the economic diversification of the region.

Culturally, Atyrau is a diverse city with a mix of Kazakh, Russian, and other ethnic groups. The population is multicultural and celebrates a number of traditional and cultural events that reflect the diversity and cultural richness of the region. The city is proud of its history and its role as an important industrial and economic center in western Kazakhstan.

The urban development of Atyrau includes modern infrastructure facilities such as roads, bridges, and Atyrau International Airport, which plays an important role in the region's air transport. The government continuously invests in improving infrastructure to support the growth of the city and improve the quality of life of its residents.

The future of Atyrau lies in the further development and modernization of its industries, the promotion of sustainable energy projects and the creation of a dynamic economic environment that meets the needs of the local population and international investors alike. Atyrau remains a key player in the global energy supply and contributes to strengthening Kazakhstan's position as a major player in the international energy market.

## Uralsk: Bridge to West Kazakhstan

Uralsk, also known as Oral, is a city in western Kazakhstan and serves as a significant cultural and economic center in the Western Kazakhstan region. Located on the banks of the Ural River, the city has a rich history dating back to the 17th century, when it was founded as a fortress to protect the southern borders of the Russian Empire.

Today, Uralsk is a modern city with a variety of industries and economic activities. Agriculture plays an important role in the local economy, with grain cultivation and livestock farming being the main activities. The city is also known for its food processing and food processing industries, which process local products and export them to other regions of Kazakhstan.

Uralsk is an important center of education and culture in western Kazakhstan. The city is home to several educational institutions, including universities and research institutes, which offer a wide range of degree programs. Culturally, Uralsk is a diverse city that reflects a mix of Kazakh, Russian, and European culture. Traditional festivals and events, such as the Maslenitsa Festival and the Nowruz Festival, are part of the city's cultural heritage and attract visitors from all over the region.

Uralsk's architecture is characterized by a mixture of historic buildings from the Tsarist era, Soviet architecture and modern buildings. The old town, with its narrow streets and historic churches, contrasts with the modern business and residential districts that characterise the cityscape. The government strives to preserve and restore historic buildings while promoting new construction projects to improve economic growth and the quality of life of residents.

The urban infrastructure includes modern transport systems such as roads, bridges and the Oral International Airport, which plays an important role in the region's air traffic. The government continuously invests in improving infrastructure to support the growth of the city and improve the quality of life of its residents.

The future of Uralsk lies in promoting sustainable development, diversifying the economy, and creating a dynamic urban environment that meets the needs of a growing population and the challenges of the 21st century. Uralsk remains a bridge to western Kazakhstan and contributes to strengthening regional integration and economic progress.

## Pavlodar: Industrial hub in the east

Pavlodar, a city in eastern Kazakhstan, plays a crucial role as an industrial hub in the region. Located on the Irtysh River, the city is known for its diverse industrial base and strategic location, which makes it an important economic center. Historically, Pavlodar was founded in the 18th century and over time developed into a significant commercial and industrial center.

The economy of Pavlodar is strongly influenced by industry, especially the chemical, petrochemical and metal processing industries. The city is home to several industrial plants and manufacturing facilities that produce a variety of products such as chemicals, fertilizers, steel, and aluminum. These industries contribute significantly to the economic development of the city and the country and provide numerous jobs for the local population.

Pavlodar is also an important center for energy production in Kazakhstan. The city is home to several power plants that generate electricity from various energy sources such as coal, natural gas, and renewables. The city's energy infrastructure plays an important role in securing the energy supply for the region's industries and population.

Culturally, Pavlodar is a diverse city with a mix of Kazakh, Russian, and other ethnic groups. The population celebrates a number of traditional festivals and cultural events that reflect the cultural diversity and heritage of the region. The city prides itself on its cultural institutions, such as theaters, museums, and art galleries, which offer an insight into the history and cultural heritage of Pavlodar.

The city's architecture is a mix of historic buildings from the Tsarist era, Soviet architecture, and modern structures. The old town with its historic buildings and churches contrasts with the modern residential and business districts that characterize the modern cityscape. The government strives to preserve and restore historic buildings while promoting new construction projects to improve economic growth and the quality of life of residents.

Pavlodar's urban infrastructure includes modern transportation systems such as roads, bridges, and Pavlodar International Airport, which plays an important role in the region's air traffic. The government continuously invests in improving infrastructure to support the growth of the city and improve the quality of life of its residents.

The future of Pavlodar lies in the further development and modernization of its industries, the promotion of sustainable energy projects and the creation of a dynamic economic environment that meets the needs of a growing population and the challenges of the 21st century. Pavlodar remains a major industrial hub in eastern Kazakhstan and contributes to strengthening the regional economy and economic progress.

# Karaganda: Mining and Industrial History

Karaganda, a significant city in central Kazakhstan, is closely linked to the country's mining and industrial history. Founded in the 19th century, the city played a key role in the development of the coal mining industry in the region. The rich coal deposits around Karaganda made the city an important center for the mining and processing of coal, which was used both for local needs and for export.

The industrial development of Karaganda was driven by the establishment of coal mines and coking plants, which formed the basis for the economic expansion of the city. The coal industry created jobs for thousands of people and contributed to urban development and population growth. In Soviet times, Karaganda was a major industrial center and an important supplier of coal for Soviet heavy industry.

Culturally, Karaganda is a diverse city with a mix of Kazakh, Russian, and other ethnic groups. The city is home to a number of cultural institutions such as theatres, museums and art galleries that offer an insight into the history and cultural heritage of the region. Traditional festivals and events are part of Karaganda's cultural life and attract visitors from all over the region.

The city's architecture is a mix of historic Soviet-era buildings, Soviet architecture, and modern structures. The old town with its old factory buildings and residential buildings contrasts with the modern business and residential districts that characterize the modern cityscape. The government strives to preserve and restore historic buildings while promoting new construction projects to improve economic growth and the quality of life of residents.

Karaganda's urban infrastructure includes modern transportation systems such as roads, bridges, and Karaganda International Airport, which plays an important role in the region's air traffic. The government continuously invests in improving infrastructure to support the growth of the city and improve the quality of life of its residents.

The future of Karaganda lies in the further development and diversification of its industries, including mining, energy and other economic sectors. The city strives to preserve its historical role as an industrial center while adapting to the challenges of the global economy and promoting sustainable development projects. Karaganda remains an important center for Kazakhstan's mining and industrial history, helping to strengthen the regional economy and economic progress.

# Aktobe: Regional diversity in the west

Aktobe, also known as Aktobe, is a city in western Kazakhstan and represents a rich variety of cultural and economic aspects in the region. Located on the Irgis River, the city is an important center for trade, education and industrial development. Founded in the 19th century, Aktobe has a long history as a strategic trading post and an important stop on the Silk Road.

Economically, Aktobe is known for its variety of industries, ranging from oil and gas production to food processing. The city is an important producer of agricultural products such as grain, cotton and livestock, which contribute to the economic base of the region. The oil and gas industry also plays a significant role in Aktobe, with several international companies operating in the region to develop and exploit the rich energy resources.

Culturally, Aktobe is a multicultural city with a population that includes a mix of Kazakh, Russian, and other ethnic groups. Traditional festivals and cultural events such as the Nowruz Festival and the Sabantuy Festival are part of the city's cultural heritage and reflect the diversity and cultural heritage of the region. The city is also home to a number of cultural institutions such as theaters, museums, and art galleries that enrich the cultural life of its residents.

Aktobe's architecture is characterized by a mix of historic buildings from the Tsarist era, Soviet architecture, and modern structures. The old town with its historic buildings and markets contrasts with the modern business and residential districts that characterize the modern cityscape. The government strives to preserve and restore historic buildings while promoting new construction projects to improve economic growth and the quality of life of residents.

Aktobe's urban infrastructure includes modern transportation systems such as roads, bridges, and Aktobe International Airport, which plays an important role in the region's air traffic. The government continuously invests in improving infrastructure to support the growth of the city and improve the quality of life of its residents.

Aktobe's future lies in further diversifying its economy and promoting sustainable development projects. The city strives to preserve its historical role as a commercial center while addressing the challenges of the 21st century. Aktobe remains an example of regional diversity in western Kazakhstan and contributes to strengthening regional integration and economic progress.

# Turkestan: Historical Heritage and Pilgrimage Site

Turkestan, also known as Turkistan, is a historic city in southern Kazakhstan and a significant cultural center of the region. The city has a long history, dating back to ancient times, when it was an important trading post on the Silk Road. Turkestan was founded in the 5th century and has been a center of culture, religion, and trade in Central Asia over the centuries.

The historical heritage of Turkestan is closely linked to the rise of the Sufi order and in particular to the mausoleum of Hodja Ahmed Yassawi. This impressive 14th-century structure is a UNESCO World Heritage Site and an important pilgrimage site for Muslims from all over the world. The mausoleum is an outstanding example of Islamic architecture, attracting thousands of pilgrims and tourists every year who appreciate the spiritual significance and artistic design of the building.

Culturally, Turkestan is a city that has preserved a rich variety of traditions and customs. The local population consists mainly of Kazakhs, but also of other ethnic groups such as Russians and Tatars. Traditional festivals and cultural events play an important role in the lives of Turkestan residents and contribute to the preservation of the region's cultural heritage.

The architecture of Turkestan is characterized by a mixture of historical buildings from the time of the rule of the Kazakh khanate, Soviet architecture and modern buildings. The old town, with its narrow streets and historic mosques, contrasts with the modern business and residential districts that characterise the modern cityscape. The government strives to preserve and restore historic buildings to preserve the city's cultural heritage while promoting new construction projects that aim to improve economic growth and the quality of life of residents.

Turkestan's urban infrastructure includes modern transportation systems such as roads, bridges, and Turkestan International Airport, which plays an important role in the region's air traffic. The government continuously invests in improving infrastructure to support the growth of the city and improve the quality of life of its residents.

The future of Turkestan lies in the further promotion of tourism, the preservation of historical heritage and the strengthening of its position as a cultural and religious center in Kazakhstan. Turkestan remains a symbol of Central Asia's rich historical heritage and cultural diversity, attracting visitors from all over the world who want to discover the history and beauty of this unique city.

# The Silk Road: Trade Route of History

One of the most famous trade routes in history, the Silk Road stretched thousands of kilometers through Central Asia, connecting the ancient civilizations of the East and the West. Its origins date back to ancient times, when caravan-like trade trains transported precious goods such as silk, spices, precious metals, and technological innovations between China, India, Persia, the Middle East, and Europe.

The Silk Road was not only a trade route, but also an important route for cultural exchange, the dissemination of religions and ideas, and the transfer of knowledge and technologies. Over centuries, the Silk Road has flourished under various empires and dominions, including the Han Dynasty in China, the Persian Empire, the Byzantine Empire, and the Roman Empire.

Flourishing trading cities and caravan stations sprang up along the Silk Road, serving as hubs for the exchange of goods and ideas. Cities such as Samarkand, Bukhara, Kashgar, Persia and Aleppo flourished as cultural and economic centers. These cities were known for their magnificent bazaars, mosques, madrasahs and palaces, which are still testimonies to their former importance.

The name "Silk Road" was coined in the 19th century by the German scholar Ferdinand von Richthofen, who recognized the historical importance of this trade route. Silk from China was one of the most precious commodities transported along the route and had a great influence on the cultures and economies along the way.

With the discovery of new sea routes in the 15th century and the expansion of European colonial powers, the Silk Road gradually lost its importance as a main artery for trade between East and West. Nevertheless, it remains a symbol of early global trade and cultural exchange between different civilizations.

Today, the Silk Road is experiencing a revival as a transcontinental trade and infrastructure initiative initiated by China and encompassing several countries in Asia, Europe and Africa. This ambitious project, known as the "One Belt, One Road" or "Belt and Road Initiative", aims to promote economic integration along the old trade routes and create new opportunities for trade, infrastructure projects and cultural exchanges.

The Silk Road thus remains not only an important historical heritage, but also a symbol of global interconnectedness and the continuous development of human civilization over the centuries.

# Modern transport infrastructure and development

Modern transport infrastructure is crucial for the economic development and growth of a region or country. In Kazakhstan, the government has made significant efforts in recent decades to modernise and expand transport infrastructure. This includes the construction of new roads, motorways and bridges, as well as the modernisation of existing transport routes to improve the mobility of people and goods.

A key element of the modern transport infrastructure in Kazakhstan is the rail network, which serves as an important transport route for freight transport. Kazakhstan has an extensive rail network that connects the country's capitals and important cities, as well as international connections to neighboring countries such as Russia, China, and Central Asia. The construction of the new railway line along the Silk Road has helped to strengthen Kazakhstan as a transit country for trade between East and West.

In addition to rail transport, road transport plays a crucial role in Kazakhstan's transport infrastructure. The development and modernisation of the road network has helped to improve connections between urban centres, rural areas and international borders. Highways such as the M-36, which crosses the country from north to south, and the M-32, which is an east-west connection, are examples of efforts to improve road infrastructure.

Another important area of modern transport infrastructure is air transport. Kazakhstan has several international airports, including Nursultan Nazarbayev Airport in the capital Nur-Sultan and Almaty Airport. These airports serve as major hubs in international air traffic, supporting both passenger and cargo flights to destinations throughout Eurasia and beyond.

The development of transport infrastructure in Kazakhstan is driven by extensive government investment and partnerships with international organisations and companies. These investments are aimed at promoting economic development, strengthening trade links and improving the quality of life of the population. Future challenges include the sustainable development of transport infrastructures, coping with increasing traffic volumes and the integration of new technologies to improve efficiency and safety in transport.

Overall, modern transport infrastructure plays a crucial role in shaping Kazakhstan's future as a regional player in the field of trade, economy and international cooperation. The continuous efforts to develop and modernise transport routes are a sign of the country's commitment to sustainable growth and development in the 21st century.

# Natural resources and environmental protection

Natural resources and environmental protection play a crucial role in Kazakhstan's economic and ecological landscape. The country is rich in natural resources, including large deposits of oil, natural gas, coal, uranium, iron, gold and other minerals. These resources form the basis of Kazakhstan's economy and contribute significantly to the country's gross domestic product. The extraction and processing of raw materials such as crude oil and natural gas plays a central role in the country's economic development, especially in the regions around Atyrau, Aksai and Tengiz.

In addition to mineral resources, Kazakhstan has a rich agricultural base that includes grains, cotton, livestock, and other agricultural products. Agriculture is a significant source of jobs and contributes to the country's food security. At the same time, the management of agricultural land and water resources poses a challenge, especially in arid and semi-arid areas of the country.

The protection of the natural environment is an increasingly important concern for the government and people of Kazakhstan. The country is affected by various environmental problems, including water pollution, soil degradation, and air pollution due to industrial activities and transportation. In recent years, the government has taken measures to improve environmental standards and promote environmentally friendly practices.

Kazakhstan is also known for its diverse nature and nature reserves. The country is home to several national parks and nature reserves that protect rich wildlife, including rare species such as the Kazakh tiger and saiga antelope. The protection of these natural habitats and their biodiversity is crucial for the conservation of biodiversity and the ecological balance in the region.

The promotion of renewable energies such as wind and solar energy is also gaining in importance in Kazakhstan. The country has great potential for renewable energy, especially in remote areas that are not connected to the national grid. Projects to develop wind farms and solar power plants contribute to the diversification of energy sources and support the goal of reducing dependence on fossil fuels.

Overall, Kazakhstan faces challenges and opportunities in terms of its natural resources and environmental protection. The sustainable use of resources and the protection of the environment are crucial for the long-term development of the country and ensuring a healthy environment for future generations. Progress in these areas will depend largely on how well government, industry and people work together to promote sustainable development and address environmental challenges.

## Steppe and semi-desert: Ecosystems of Kazakhstan

The steppe and semi-desert are two important ecosystems that shape the landscape of Kazakhstan and are home to a diverse flora and fauna. The steppe stretches over large parts of northern and central Kazakhstan and is characterized by an open, treeless grassland. Grasses such as feather grass, meadow panicle grass and fescue grass dominate here, which have adapted to the dry and continental conditions of the region. The steppe is home to a variety of animal species, including mammals such as saiga antelopes, gazelles, wolves, foxes, and marmots, as well as birds such as steppe eagles, quails, and larks.

The semi-desert, also known as Chaparal or Semidesert, includes areas in southern and southwestern Kazakhstan that are characterized by low rainfall and extreme temperature fluctuations. Characteristic of the semi-desert are drought-resistant plants such as salt steppes, desert grasses and shrubs such as tamarisk and salt bush. These plants are adapted to the scarce water resources and form important habitats for animals such as the saiga antelope, jackals, foxes and various rodents.

Both ecosystems play an essential role in Kazakhstan's ecological balance and are important for the conservation of biodiversity in the region. They provide habitat and food for a variety of animals, birds and plants that are adapted to the extreme conditions of the continental arid landscapes. The preservation of these ecosystems is crucial for the sustainable use of the country's natural resources and the protection of its unique environment.

The steppe and semi-desert are also culturally significant for Kazakhstan, as they support traditional ways of life and nomadic traditions. Historically, the vast open grasslands of the steppe were the habitat of the nomadic peoples of Central Asia, who raised cattle and lived in yurts. Today, these regions are also popular destinations for ecotourism and nature observation, as they offer visitors the opportunity to experience the unspoiled beauty and unique wildlife of these landscapes.

The challenges for the conservation of these ecosystems include the sustainable management of pastureland, protection against overgrazing and the management of environmental changes such as climate change and land degradation. By protecting and sustainably using the steppe and semi-desert, Kazakhstan can preserve its natural environment while promoting economic development based on the country's natural resources.

# Wildlife and nature reserves

Kazakhstan's wildlife is as diverse as its landscapes and includes an abundance of animal species that are native to the steppes and semi-deserts as well as the mountainous regions and forest areas of the country. One of the most famous animal species is the saiga antelope, which lives in the open steppe landscapes of the central and southern regions. This antelope species is known for its distinctive curved nose and plays an important ecological role as a herbivore.

Another characteristic animal species is the Kazakh tiger, a subspecies of the Siberian tiger that can be found in the forested areas of eastern Kazakhstan. These majestic big cats are highly endangered and are under conservation measures to preserve and stabilize their populations. Other predators found in Kazakhstan include wolves, lynxes, foxes, and brown bears that live in the country's mountainous regions and forests.

A wide variety of fish species can be found in Kazakhstan's waterways, including the Caspian Sea and the country's numerous rivers and lakes. Among the most common are the sturgeon, zander, carp species and various species of trout. These fish are not only important for the ecological balance of the waters, but also play a role in the country's fishing economy.

In addition to land and aquatic life, Kazakhstan is also home to a variety of migratory birds that rest or nest along the Silk Road and in the country's wetlands. This makes Kazakhstan an important hub for bird migration and a destination for ornithologists from all over the world who study the diversity of bird species and their migrations.

Nature reserves play a central role in the protection of Kazakhstan's wildlife. The country has several national parks and nature reserves that protect various ecosystems and endangered species. These include the Altyn Emel National Park, the Ile-Alatau National Park and the Korgalzhyn Nature Reserve, which is recognized as a UNESCO World Heritage Site for its wetlands and the migratory birds that live in them.

The challenges for nature conservation in Kazakhstan include the sustainable use of natural resources, the fight against poaching and illegal hunting, and the management of environmental problems such as habitat loss and climate change. Through international cooperation and the implementation of effective conservation measures, Kazakhstan strives to preserve its unique wildlife and leave an intact nature for future generations.

# Culinary traditions and national dishes

Kazakhstan's culinary traditions reflect the diversity of its cultures and the historical influences of the Silk Road. The nomadic roots of Kazakh society, which have shaped its eating habits for centuries, play a central role in this. Traditional dishes are often robust and nutritious, designed for life in the vast steppe landscapes of Central Asia.

An outstanding feature of Kazakh cuisine is the use of meat, especially sheep and horse meat. The horse meat is often made into "beshbarmak", a traditional dish consisting of thin flatbreads of dough and boiled meat, often served with onions and a special sauce. Sheep meat can be found in various ways of preparation, including stews such as "Zharkop" or grilled on skewers ("Shashlik").

Dairy products also play an important role in the Kazakh diet. "Kumis", fermented mare's milk, is a traditional drink that has both health-promoting properties and cultural significance. Yoghurt ("Kurt") and sour milk ("Ayran") are other popular products that are often served with meals or eaten as a snack in between.

The use of cereal products is also widespread. "Baursak", deep-fried dough balls, are a popular snack that is served on various occasions. Pasta such as "nan" (bread) and "lepeshka" (flatbread) are staples that are served with almost every meal.

Vegetables and fruits play a rather limited role in traditional Kazakh cuisine, although seasonal products such as carrots, potatoes, and various types of berries are used in some dishes. Influences from Russian and Uzbek cuisine are also noticeable, especially in regions historically linked to these cultures.

The culinary diversity of Kazakhstan reflects not only its geographical location and historical traditions, but also the hospitality and generosity of its inhabitants. Meals are often social occasions where family and friends come together to enjoy the rich tradition and flavors of Kazakh cuisine. International cuisine influences are also noticeable in the cities, resulting in a culinary fusion that is both traditional and modern.

# Famous Kazakh dishes and specialties

In Kazakhstan, there are a variety of famous dishes and specialties that reflect both the traditional cuisine and the cultural influences of the region. One of the most famous dishes is "Beshbarmak", which literally translates to "five fingers". It consists of thin flatbreads of dough served with boiled meat (typically sheep or horse) and onions. This dish is not only a culinary specialty, but also a symbol of hospitality and conviviality in Kazakhstan.

Another popular dish is "zharkop", a spicy meat stew that is often made with potatoes and carrots. Meat lovers also appreciate "shashlik", grilled meat (usually lamb or beef) served on skewers and often enjoyed on festive occasions.

Dairy products play an important role in Kazakh cuisine. "Kumis", fermented mare's milk, is not only a traditional drink, but also a symbol of health and well-being. "Kurt", a type of dry yoghurt, is often served as a snack or side dish with bread and is particularly popular with nomadic peoples.

In the southern regions of Kazakhstan, which border closer to Central Asia, pasta such as "samsa" (stuffed dumplings) and "belyash" (deep-fried dough pies) are popular. These dishes show influences from Uzbek and Turkish cuisine, which were shaped by the trade relations along the historic Silk Road.

In addition to the main courses, Kazakh desserts and desserts are also worth mentioning. "Baursak", deep-fried dough balls, are often served on special occasions such as weddings and holidays. Honey, dried fruits and nuts are often used in traditional desserts that have a long history and often pass on family recipes.

The diversity of Kazakh cuisine reflects not only the country's natural resources, but also the cultural diversity and historical influences that have shaped it. The preservation and transmission of these culinary traditions is an important part of Kazakhstan's cultural identity and a source of national pride and cohesion.

# Music and Dance: Cultural Expressions

Kazakh music and dance are deeply rooted in the country's history and traditions, reflecting the cultural diversity and nomadic roots of the population. The traditional music of Kazakhstan is often accompanied by instruments such as the "dombra", a two-stringed lute known for its clear sound and often played by storytellers and bards. The dombra is not only a musical instrument, but also a symbol of Kazakh identity and is often played at festivals and cultural events.

Another traditional form of music is the "kui", an instrumental piece often played by "küis" (musicians) who show a high level of virtuoso technique and creative improvisation. Heavily influenced by nomadic culture, the Kui can reflect different moods and landscapes, from the vastness of the steppe to the majestic mountains of the country.

In addition to instrumental music, singing traditions are also deeply rooted. Kazakh folk songs called "zhirens" are often epic and tell of heroism, love of nature and the nomadic way of life. These songs are often performed in groups or by soloists and are an important part of the oral tradition and cultural transmission in Kazakhstan.

Traditional Kazakh dance is as diverse as the music. A well-known dance style is the "Kara Zhorga", which is performed by men in traditional costumes and includes acrobatic elements as well as powerful steps. "Zhigitovka" is another dance style that emphasizes the dexterity and strength of male dancers and is often seen at celebrations such as weddings and festivals.

Women often dance the "Kara Zhorga" in an adapted form or perform the "Aitys", a poetic competition accompanied by movements and gestures. The traditional dances of Kazakhstan are not only artistic expressions, but also means of celebrating community and strengthening cultural ties between generations.

Modern influences have also shaped Kazakh music and dance, especially through pop music and international styles popular in urban centers of the country. Nevertheless, traditional music and the art of dance remain an integral part of Kazakhstan's cultural identity, which is proudly maintained and passed on in order to preserve the uniqueness and diversity of Kazakh culture.

## Literature and the art scene

Kazakhstan's literary and artistic scene is characterized by a rich tradition and a variety of creative expressions that reflect both local and international influences. In the Soviet era, literature played a central role in the country's cultural development, with writers such as Mukhtar Auezov and Abai Kunanbayev gaining national and international recognition. Her works often deal with historical and social issues and have helped to cement Kazakhstan's identity.

With Kazakhstan's independence, the literary scene has evolved, giving rise to new currents that embrace modern themes and contemporary approaches. Authors such as Olzhas Suleimenov and Dulat Isabekov have enriched the Kazakh literary landscape with works that address current social and political challenges, while preserving traditional narrative forms and styles.

The art scene in Kazakhstan is also vibrant and diverse. The traditional art of the Kazakh nomads, such as the production of carpets ("shyrdak") and felt products, has a long history and is still appreciated today. Modern art forms, including painting, sculpture, and installations, have flourished strongly in the country's urban centers, with artists such as Moldakul Narymbetov and Almagul Menlibayeva gaining international recognition.

The Kazakh art scene also benefits from increasing international networking and exchange with other cultures. Art galleries and exhibitions in cities such as Almaty and Astana (now Nur-Sultan) provide platforms for local and international artists to showcase their work to a wide audience and promote cultural dialogue.

In addition to literature and the visual arts, traditional music plays an important role in the cultural landscape of Kazakhstan. The "Akyns", traditional storytellers and bards, contribute to the oral tradition and cultural identity of the country by sharing stories of heroism, love and nature through their songs and tales.

Overall, Kazakhstan's literary and artistic scene reflects the country's diversity and deep-rooted cultural traditions, while also facing the challenges of modernity and promoting new forms of expression and innovation.

# Festivals and holidays

Festivals and holidays play an important role in the cultural and social life of Kazakhstan and reflect the diversity of ethnic groups as well as the historical and religious traditions of the country. One of the most important holidays is Nowruz, the Persian New Year, which is celebrated by many ethnic groups in Kazakhstan. It marks the beginning of spring and is celebrated with traditional dances, feasts and the exchange of gifts. Nowruz is not only a celebration of nature and new beginnings, but also a symbol of cultural solidarity across ethnic boundaries.

Another important holiday is the Republic of Kazakhstan Day on December 16, which celebrates the anniversary of the country's independence from the Soviet Union in 1991. This day is celebrated with solemn events, parades, and cultural events across the country to celebrate Kazakhstan's national unity and progress.

Religious holidays such as Eid al-Fitr and Eid al-Adha are also of great importance to the Muslim population of Kazakhstan and are celebrated with prayers, feasts and the distribution of alms. These holidays are occasions for family and community to gather and pray together.

May 9 is another important holiday in Kazakhstan that honors World War II Victory Day over Nazi Germany and its allies. This day is marked with military parades, floral laying at war memorials and commemorative events in memory of the fallen soldiers.

In addition to these national and religious holidays, there are also regional festivals and customs that reflect the diversity of cultural traditions in Kazakhstan. For example, the annual "Kazakh Eli" festival is celebrated in Astana (now Nur-Sultan), which includes a variety of cultural events, concerts, and exhibitions to celebrate the country's heritage and cultural diversity.

In rural areas, traditional festivals such as the "Nauryz" festival, which marks the beginning of spring, are often celebrated with horse races, games and traditional food. These festivals are an opportunity for the community to come together, cultivate ancient customs and preserve the rich cultural history of Kazakhstan.

Overall, festivals and holidays in Kazakhstan are not only occasions for celebration and entertainment, but also important expressions of national identity, cultural diversity and cohesion in Kazakh society. They show the country's deep-rooted traditions and values and contribute to strengthening social cohesion.

## Sports and leisure activities

Sports and leisure activities are of great importance in Kazakhstan and reflect the diversity of landscapes and the cultural preferences of the population. An important sport in Kazakhstan is traditional equestrian sports, especially horse racing, which has a long tradition and can often be seen at festivals and celebrations. These races, known as "Kokpar" or "Ulak Tartys", are not only sporting competitions, but also an opportunity for the community to demonstrate their skill and strength.

Another popular sport in Kazakhstan is wrestling, known as "Kazakh Kuresi", which dates back to a centuries-old tradition and requires a combination of skill, strength and strategy. Wrestling matches are often held at national festivals such as Nowruz or Independence Day celebrations, attracting both participants and spectators from all over the region.

In the field of winter sports, Kazakhstan has produced a growing number of winter sports enthusiasts, especially in skiing and ice sports. Ski resorts such as Shymbulak near Almaty and Akbulak near Astana offer world-class slopes and facilities for skiers and snowboarders. Winter sports have become a popular leisure activity, attracting both local enthusiasts and international guests looking for the challenge of the Kazakh mountains. Basketball and volleyball are also popular sports in Kazakhstan, played at both professional and amateur levels. The Kazakh Basketball League (KBL) and the Volleyball League (KVL) are highly developed and have produced numerous talented players who are internationally successful. These sports are promoted in schools, universities, and sports clubs across the country to support young athletes and further increase the popularity of the sport.

In addition to traditional sports, Kazakhstan also has a growing fitness and wellness culture, which is promoted by modern gyms, sports halls and yoga studios. Cities such as Almaty and Astana offer a variety of recreational opportunities, including hiking, cycling, and water sports on the country's numerous lakes and rivers.

Overall, the variety of sports and leisure activities in Kazakhstan reflects the dynamic nature of the country, where tradition and modernity come together harmoniously. These activities are not only an expression of the physical fitness and competitive spirit of the population, but also an opportunity to enjoy the natural beauties and cultural treasures of Kazakhstan.

# Nomadic culture and traditional way of life

The nomadic culture and traditional way of life in Kazakhstan have a long and deep-rooted history that dates back to prehistoric times. The Kazakh nomads are known for their ability to adapt to the harsh landscape of the steppes and semi-deserts that dominate the country. For a long time, this way of life was central to the survival strategies and social organization of the population.

Traditionally, the Kazakh nomads were organized in tribal associations, which were led by councils of elders and had a strict hierarchy and clear social rules. Their main activity was livestock breeding, especially the keeping of horses, cattle, sheep and goats. The nomads moved their herds from one pasture to the next, using seasonal migration routes to open up fertile pastures and make the most of natural resources.

The traditional Kazakh yurt, known as "Yurta" or "Kazakh", was and still is the characteristic dwelling of the nomads. This round portable tent structure is made of a wooden frame covered with felt, which provides protection from the extreme climatic conditions of the steppe in both summer and winter. The yurt serves not only as a dwelling, but also as a social hub for family affairs, celebrations, and cultural activities.

The nomadic way of life has left a rich cultural heritage, which is reflected in the traditional music, dances, festivals and handicrafts of the Kazakh people. Musical instruments such as the dombra and the kobyz are characteristic of the Kazakh musical tradition and are often played on festive occasions to celebrate the connection with nature and the spiritual dimension of nomadic life.

With the development of modern society and urbanization, many Kazakhs have abandoned their traditional nomadic lifestyle and become sedentary. Nevertheless, nomadic culture remains an important part of Kazakhstan's national identity and is actively nurtured and promoted through cultural programs, museums and events such as the "Nomad Games" festival.

More recently, some nomadic families have decided to revisit parts of their traditional way of life and integrate certain aspects into their modern lives. This is often done out of a desire to preserve the old traditions and to pass on to the younger generations the values and skills of their ancestors.

Kazakhstan's nomadic culture and traditional way of life not only offer a glimpse into the country's history and cultural diversity, but are also a living heritage that highlights the resilience and adaptability of the Kazakh population over the centuries.

# Fine Arts and Crafts

The visual arts and crafts of Kazakhstan reflect a rich cultural tradition that encompasses both local influences and international currents. The history of Kazakh art goes back a long way and has developed over centuries, starting with prehistoric rock carvings and cave paintings discovered in different regions of the country. These early works of art provide insight into the lives and beliefs of the early inhabitants of Kazakhstan and are a valuable cultural heritage.

An important period for the development of Kazakh art was the Islamic era, which began in the 8th century. Under the influence of Islam, impressive architectural works such as mosques, mausoleums and madrasahs were created in Kazakhstan, often decorated with elaborate tiles, carvings and stucco decorations. These buildings are not only religious centers, but also masterpieces of Islamic art and architecture that are still admired today.

Traditional Kazakh art is strongly influenced by the nomadic way of life and the natural conditions of the region. In the past, carpet weaving, felting, pottery and metalwork were important crafts that were passed down from generation to generation. The artisans used local materials such as wool, leather, wood, and copper to create artistic and functional items that served both practical and aesthetic purposes.

Over time, Kazakh art continued to evolve and incorporate influences from other cultures, especially Russia and Europe. This led to a variety of styles and techniques in painting, sculpture and graphics. Modern Kazakh artists and artisans are experimenting with new materials and expressions, while respecting and preserving the traditional roots of their art.

Kazakhstan has a vibrant art scene with numerous galleries, museums and art schools that help preserve and promote the country's artistic heritage. Modern art festivals and exhibitions attract both national and international artists and provide a platform for cultural exchange and the further development of the contemporary art scene.

The visual arts and crafts of Kazakhstan are not only an expression of creative talents, but also a window into the country's history, culture and identity. They play an important role in preserving cultural heritage, inspiring new generations and promoting the diversity of artistic expressions in Kazakhstan.

# Modern pop culture and media landscape

Kazakhstan's modern pop culture and media landscape have evolved greatly in recent decades, reflecting both global trends and local idiosyncrasies. Kazakhstan, as a multi-ethnic and multicultural state, is experiencing dynamic development in the fields of music, film, television, fashion and digital media.

In the music scene, Kazakh artists and bands have gained an increasing presence in recent years. Local pop stars such as Dimash Kudaibergen have gained international recognition and contribute to the popularity of Kazakh music. The variety of genres ranges from traditional Kazakh music to modern pop music and electronic sounds that reflect both local and international influences.

The film sector in Kazakhstan has also developed, with Kazakh films attracting attention at international film festivals. Directors such as Darezhan Omirbayev and Emir Baigazin have shaped the Kazakh cinema landscape with their works and dealt with topics such as identity, history and social challenges. The support of state and private initiatives promotes the production and distribution of Kazakh films, which are increasingly attracting international attention.

Kazakhstan's media landscape is characterised by a mixture of state-controlled and independent media. Freedom of the press is an issue of growing importance, with independent media increasingly creating space for critical reporting and freedom of expression. Online platforms and social media play an important role in spreading news and information among the population, especially among the younger generation.

The fashion industry in Kazakhstan is also experiencing a renaissance, with Kazakh designers attracting national and international attention. Fashion shows and design competitions promote the creativity and diversity of Kazakh fashion, which combines traditional elements with modern trends. Kazakhstani models and influencers are present on social media and contribute to the spread of Kazakh fashion and styles.

The digital media landscape in Kazakhstan is growing rapidly, with internet use and smartphone penetration increasing. Online platforms, streaming services and digital content are gaining popularity and offer a variety of entertainment and educational opportunities for the population. Kazakhstan bloggers, vloggers, and influencers have an active presence on social media and help shape the country's digital culture.

In conclusion, Kazakhstan's modern pop culture and media landscape are a reflection of the country's diversity and dynamism. Not only do they provide entertainment and artistic expression, but they also play an important role in promoting cultural identity and national pride in a globalized world.

# Kazakhstan in global diplomacy

Kazakhstan plays an important role in global diplomacy, shaped by its geopolitical position, its membership in international organizations and its efforts to promote peace and security. As the largest Central Asian country and former Soviet republic, Kazakhstan has pursued an active foreign policy since its independence in 1991.

A central point in Kazakhstan's diplomatic strategy is its role as a mediator and host of international dialogues and negotiations. Astana, now Nur-Sultan, became an important venue for international conferences and summits. The format of the "Astana talks", which deal with the resolution of the Syrian conflict, is particularly well known. These efforts have helped establish Kazakhstan as a neutral and trustworthy mediator in global affairs.

Kazakhstan is a member of a number of international organizations, including the United Nations, the Organization for Security and Co-operation in Europe (OSCE), and the Shanghai Cooperation Organization (SCO). These memberships allow Kazakhstan to participate in global decision-making processes and represent its interests on the international stage.

Another important area of Kazakh diplomacy is the promotion of economic cooperation and trade relations. The country has bilateral and multilateral agreements with various states and regions worldwide to attract investment and promote trade. Relations with Russia, China, the United States and EU countries are particularly important.

Kazakhstan is also actively engaged in nuclear non-proliferation and played a crucial role in abandoning the world's third-largest nuclear arsenal after the collapse of the Soviet Union. This led to the establishment of the Semipalatinsk nuclear weapons test site and strengthened Kazakhstan's commitment to a world without nuclear weapons.

With regard to regional security issues, Kazakhstan strives to promote a stable and peaceful neighbourhood policy. It works closely with its Central Asian neighbors and participates in regional forums such as the Organization for Economic Cooperation (EAEU) and the Central Asian Economic Union (CAEU).

Kazakhstan's strategic importance as a bridge between Europe and Asia, as well as a gateway to Central Asia's rich resources, has a significant influence on his diplomatic efforts. The country strives to pursue a balanced and pragmatic foreign policy based on dialogue, cooperation and mutual respect in order to further strengthen its position in global diplomacy.

# International Relations and Partnerships

Kazakhstan maintains diverse international relations and partnerships that span both regional and global dimensions. Since gaining independence in 1991, the country has pursued an active foreign policy to strengthen its position in the global arena and promote economic and political ties.

At the regional level, Kazakhstan is a key player in Central Asia and works closely with its neighbours in the region. Membership in organizations such as the Shanghai Cooperation Organization (SCO) and the Organization for Economic Cooperation (EAEU) underscores his efforts for regional integration and security. Through bilateral agreements and initiatives, Kazakhstan promotes economic cooperation, infrastructure projects and the exchange of resources such as energy and water in the region.

At the global level, Kazakhstan is actively involved in international forums and organizations. As a member of the United Nations, it plays a role in global security, development aid and human rights issues. The country has also been committed to promoting nuclear non-proliferation and hosted the Semipalatinsk nuclear weapons test site, the closure of which made a significant contribution to global security.

Kazakhstan has diplomatic relations with a wide range of countries around the world, including major powers such as the United States, Russia, China, and the European Union. These partnerships aim to promote trade and investment, facilitate cultural exchanges and represent strategic interests at the international level. Economic cooperation includes energy projects, mining, agriculture and technology, further strengthening Kazakhstan's role as a bridge between Europe and Asia.

In multilateral diplomacy, Kazakhstan is also involved in various initiatives to resolve conflicts and promote global development goals. It is known for its efforts in the field of sustainable development, especially with regard to environmental protection and resource management. These initiatives help to consolidate Kazakhstan's international reputation as a reliable partner and facilitator.

In conclusion, Kazakhstan pursues a dynamic and multifaceted foreign policy based on the promotion of peace, security and economic cooperation. Through its participation in regional and global initiatives, the country strives to strengthen its strategic position and contribute to a stable and prosperous world order.

# Tourism: Sights and Destinations

Kazakhstan offers a variety of fascinating sights and destinations that include both historical and natural treasures. One of the country's most recognizable landmarks is the Baikonur Cosmodrome, the world's first and largest spaceport. This place has played a significant role in the history of space travel, attracting visitors from all over the world who want to explore the historical heritage of Soviet space travel.

In addition to Baikonur, Kazakhstan offers a rich historical landscape with archaeological sites such as Otrar and Sauran providing insight into the ancient history of the region. These cities were once thriving trading centers on the famous Silk Road, facilitating cultural exchanges between East and West.

The modern capital of Nur-Sultan (formerly Astana) is an architectural marvel that impresses with its futuristic skyline and iconic buildings such as the Bayterek Tower and the Baiterek Monument. The city also serves as a cultural center with museums, theaters, and concert halls that offer a glimpse into contemporary Kazakh art and culture. Almaty, the former capital, is another significant destination with a mix of Soviet architecture and modern city life. Surrounded by the majestic peaks of the Tian Shan Mountains, Almaty attracts visitors with its ski resorts in winter and its green parks and gardens in summer. For nature lovers, Kazakhstan offers stunning landscapes such as Charyn Canyon, often referred to as the "Kazakh Grand Canyon." With its bizarre rock formations and steep gorges, Charyn Canyon is a paradise for hikers and adventurers.

Lake Balkhash, one of the largest inland lakes in the world, is another impressive natural wonder of Kazakhstan. It offers not only stunning scenery, but also abundant fish stocks and unique wildlife that attract birdwatchers and nature lovers alike.

Not to mention the traditional Kazakh yurts, nomadic culture, and steppe heritage that take visitors to remote regions of the country. These authentic experiences offer a glimpse into the traditional life of the Kazakhs and their close connection with nature.

In conclusion, Kazakhstan is a fascinating destination for travelers from all over the world, with its variety of historical sites, architectural wonders, natural beauties, and cultural experiences. The combination of history, nature and hospitality makes the country an unforgettable destination in Central Asia.

## Must-see: National parks and natural wonders

Kazakhstan is home to a variety of national parks and natural wonders that attract visitors from all over the world. One of the most famous and impressive is the Altyn-Emel National Park in the southeast of the country. This area encompasses a diverse landscape of deserts and mountains and is home to the famous "Singing Dune", a huge sand dune whose sand produces sounds in certain conditions.

Another notable natural wonder is Kolsai Lake National Park, known for its three emerald mountain lakes surrounded by dense forests and alpine meadows. The park offers excellent hiking opportunities and abundant wildlife, including rare bird species.

Charyn Canyon, often referred to as the "Kazakh Grand Canyon," is another must-see. This huge gorge stretches over a length of about 80 kilometers and impresses with its bizarre rock formations and steep walls. Particularly impressive is the Valley of Castles area, known for its unusually shaped rocks.

The Ile-Alatau National Park, located near the city of Almaty, offers spectacular alpine landscapes, crystal-clear mountain lakes and a rich variety of flora and fauna. This park is a popular destination for mountain hikers, climbers, and nature lovers who want to experience the beauty of the Tian Shan Mountains.

Not to forget Lake Balkhash, one of the largest inland lakes in the world. This salt lake is known for its unique ecology and its importance as a resting place for migratory birds. The surroundings of the lake offer a fascinating landscape of deserts, steppes and semi-deserts.

In addition to these national parks and natural wonders, Kazakhstan also offers other unique landscapes such as the Betpak-Dala semi-desert and the vast plains of the Kazakh steppe that form the heart of the country.

Overall, Kazakhstan is rich in natural treasures that appeal to both adventurers and nature lovers. The diversity of landscapes and unspoiled nature make the country a fascinating destination for visitors who want to discover the beauty and diversity of Central Asia.

## Museums and historical sites

Kazakhstan is rich in historical sites and museums that reflect the rich cultural and historical development of the country. One of the most important museums is the Central Museum of the Republic of Kazakhstan in the capital Nur-Sultan. It houses an extensive collection of artifacts from different periods of Kazakhstan's history, including prehistoric finds, traditional artworks, and artifacts from the Silk Road era.

Another outstanding museum is the Historical Museum in Almaty, which also presents a wide range of exhibits on the history of Kazakhstan. Particularly noteworthy are the archaeological finds from the Bronze Age and objects from the Soviet Union.

Almaty is also home to the Central State Museum of the Republic of Kazakhstan, which is known for its extensive collection of both historical and cultural artifacts. The museum is dedicated to the preservation and presentation of Kazakh culture from antiquity to the present day.

The city of Taras, named after the legendary hero of Kazakhstan, is also known for its museum dedicated to the life and deeds of

Taras Shevchenko. It offers a deep insight into the heritage and cultural traditions of Kazakh folk art.

For lovers of archaeological sites, Kazakhstan also offers a wealth of historical sites. The ancient city of Otrar was a major trading center on the Silk Road and offers insight into the early history of the region. Other important archaeological sites include Sauran, a medieval town near Turkestan, and the ruins of Akyrtas, which reflect a mysterious and fascinating past.

In conclusion, with its plethora of museums and historical sites, Kazakhstan offers visitors the opportunity to delve deep into the country's rich history and culture. These places are not only the sites of significant historical events, but also testimonies to the cultural diversity and heritage of Kazakhstan.

# Outlook: Future prospects and challenges

Kazakhstan faces a multitude of future prospects and challenges that will shape the country in the coming decades. One of the key issues is economic diversification. The country, which has long been heavily dependent on the extraction and export of raw materials, is striving for a broader economic base. This includes investing in industries such as technology, renewable energy and agriculture to reduce dependence on oil and gas and create new revenue streams.

Another important goal is to promote education and innovation. Kazakhstan is investing heavily in educational reforms and the development of universities and research institutions to build a knowledge-based economy. This is intended to help promote talent in the state and strengthen innovative strength in order to meet the requirements of a globalised global economy.

Infrastructure modernization is also crucial. Kazakhstan is developing its transport routes, including road, rail and air transport links, to improve logistical efficiency and promote regional integration. This is particularly important as the country plays a central role as a link between Europe and Asia, especially under the new Belt and Road Initiative.

In terms of social development, Kazakhstan strives to improve the quality of life of its citizens. These include measures to combat poverty and strengthen social security systems. The promotion of health care and access to education are also priority goals in order to improve living conditions in all parts of the country.

At the global level, Kazakhstan aspires to play an active role in international affairs and multilateral organizations. The country is a member of various international bodies and seeks partnerships and collaborations with other countries worldwide. This includes the promotion of peace and security, as well as cooperation in areas such as environmental protection, climate change and sustainable development.

Despite these prospects, the country also faces challenges. This includes economic adaptation to volatile commodity markets, addressing social inequalities and ensuring sustainable development in harmony with the environment. The country's geopolitical position between major regional powers requires a balanced foreign policy and the ability to navigate international tensions.

Overall, Kazakhstan is in a period of change and transformation, characterized by its rich history and cultural diversity. Future developments will largely depend on how the country uses its resources and potential to improve the quality of life of its citizens and consolidate its role in the global community.

# Closing remarks

In this book, we have taken a comprehensive journey through the diversity and depth of Kazakhstan, a country shaped by its rich history, impressive landscapes and diverse cultures. From the vast steppes and semi-deserts in the south to the majestic mountain ranges in the east, Kazakhstan offers a natural diversity that is both fascinating and unique.

The country's history goes back deep, shaped by nomadic cultures that shaped the landscape and promoted trade along the Silk Road for centuries. With the arrival of Islam in the 8th century, a new era of cultural development began, which has left its mark on architecture, art and way of life to this day.

Kazakhstan's transition from the Soviet Union to independence in 1991 marked a turning point in its modern history. Since then, the country has undergone an impressive economic transformation, placing a central role in its natural resources such as oil, gas, and mining. At the same time, Kazakhstan has placed a strong focus on diversifying its economy to reduce dependence on commodity exports and promote new growth areas such as technology and agriculture.

Kazakhstan's cultural diversity is reflected in its ethnic groups, including Kazakhs, Russians, Uzbeks, Tatars, and many others, who together form a rich and diverse cultural landscape. This diversity is evident not only in the language and religion, but also in the country's traditional clothing, customs and culinary traditions.

The capitals of Almaty and Astana (Nur-Sultan), as well as cities such as Shymkent and Atyrau, play a central role in the country's economic and cultural life. They are not only major commercial centers, but also cultural hubs that offer a wealth of historical and modern sights.

Kazakhstan prides itself on its educational and research institutions, which produce a growing number of talented professionals and form the basis for future innovation and progress. The country's education system is committed to providing broad and high-quality education that lays the foundation for a knowledge-based economy.

The future of Kazakhstan faces challenges and opportunities in equal measure. Promoting sustainable development, protecting the environment and addressing social challenges will be key issues as the country continues to expand its role in global diplomacy and economic integration.

In conclusion, Kazakhstan shows itself to be a country with a rich past, a dynamic present and a promising future. May this book help to explore and understand the beauty and diversity of this fascinating country.

Printed in Great Britain
by Amazon